EASY PIANO

MOVIE SONGS

FOR KIDS

ISBN 978-1-5400-9739-2

For all works contained herein:
Unauthorized copying, arranging, adapting, recording, internet posting, public performance,
or other distribution of the music in this publication is an infringement of copyright.
Infringers are liable under the law.

Visit Hal Leonard Online at
www.halleonard.com

Contact us:
Hal Leonard
7777 West Bluemound Road
Milwaukee, WI 53213
Email: info@halleonard.com

In Europe, contact:
Hal Leonard Europe Limited
42 Wigmore Street
Marylebone, London, W1U 2RN
Email: info@halleonardeurope.com

In Australia, contact:
Hal Leonard Australia Pty. Ltd.
4 Lentara Court
Cheltenham, Victoria, 3192 Australia
Email: info@halleonard.com.au

T0105930

CONTENTS

★ ★ ★ ★ ★

SONG NOTES

Beyond the Sea

You can hear Robbie Williams singing this swing classic from the 1940s over the end credits of the 2003 Disney-Pixar hit *Finding Nemo*. As you begin to learn this arrangement, start with the left hand. The groovy bass line provides the framework for the right-hand tied notes and the quarter-note triplets. A quarter-note triplet is played in the time of one half note, so stretch those quarter notes out, letting the lyrics move you along.

Can't Stop the Feeling

This disco-pop song is sung in the 2016 mega-hit *Trolls*. Right hand uses the ledger line notes A and G below middle C. Those ledger lines can look tricky to read but once you've identified them, you'll be all set. Left hand has a repeating pattern of 5ths and 7ths. Looking ahead and identifying how the music is put together makes learning music easy. "Dance, dance, dance" your way through the chorus, mindful of the repeated notes in the right hand accompanied by 5ths in the left hand, and enjoy this upbeat, feel-good tune.

Theme from E.T. (The Extra Terrestrial)

The theme from Universal Pictures' 1982 science fiction classic *E.T. (The Extra-Terrestrial)* presents us with a melody that is both soulful and heroic. John Williams uses accidentals (sharps and flats not in the key signature) and a wide range to create emotion and beautiful tone color. In measure 45 left hand is notated in treble clef; be prepared to move higher on the keyboard. In measure 70 the *8va* sign means to play those notes an octave higher, and the scales beginning in measure 72 are not as difficult as they may look; that scale pattern in thirds repeats four times. As you reach the dramatic conclusion, the slanted lines between the staves show that left hand moves from treble to bass in measures 79–80.

Everything Is Awesome (Awesome Remixx!!!)

This upbeat and remarkably cheerful tune is from the 2014 animated film *The Lego Movie*. The tempo is marked "Moderately fast" and you will want enough energy to carry through with a bit of style and drive. Keep the beat going through the syncopation in measures 9–20. If you keep a steady quarter note beat (try counting out loud or tapping your foot as you play) you'll know exactly where the right-hand notes fall. Note the key change in measure 21 for the final refrain. It's awesome!

Happy

This up-tempo tune was written and sung by Pharrell Williams on the 2013 *Despicable Me 2* movie soundtrack. The song received numerous awards and was the #1 selling song the following year. Enjoy the jazzy bass line that first appears in measures 4–5. That "happy" little riff is repeated two more times before a duet breaks out in measure 18. Spend some time getting familiar with the left hand and be sure to play that part confidently against the right-hand tied notes. Look for patterns in both hands in measures 34–48; lots of repeated material there before you end with the return of the duet.

How Far I'll Go

This power ballad was sung by the title character in Disney's 2016 animated feature film *Moana*. It was written by Lin-Manuel Miranda and sung in the film by Auli'i Cravalho and recorded by Alessia Cara for the soundtrack. This melody is syncopated, with tied and dotted notes throughout. Consider tapping the rhythm and writing in the quarter-note beats as you learn this at a slow tempo. Moana is telling a story, so don't let the tempo get too fast.

I See the Light

This beautiful love theme is from Disney's 2010 animated feature film *Tangled*. Play this lyrical right-hand melody with a legato, singing tone. Take time to let the dotted rhythms move gently with the lyrics, maybe even singing along as you play. The left hand provides a simple, steady foundation.

Immortals

"Immortals" was written and performed by the rock band Fall Out Boy for the 2014 Walt Disney Animation Studios film *Big Hero 6*. Set a steady quarter-note beat before you begin. You'll want to play the eighth notes evenly and be ready to subdivide to 16th notes smoothly when they occur. Notice that the left-hand part has a few guideposts along the way. For example, in the beginning anchor yourself around middle C, played in every measure until measure 11. Now look for low A. How many times does low A appear in the next section? Analyzing the music in this way will help you learn the song more quickly.

Into the Unknown

This emotional ballad is sung by the character Elsa in the 2019 Disney animated feature *Frozen 2*. Notice the $\frac{12}{8}$ time signature. You could count twelve eighth notes per measure, but it's easier to count four dotted quarter notes per measure. To see this clearly, look at the left-hand part in measures 15–22. Those dotted quarter note beats provide a framework for the right-hand melody. Write in these larger beats in other measures if you find it helpful. If you are unfamiliar with this song, listen to a recording to hear the four larger beats within the $\frac{12}{8}$ time signature.

Linus and Lucy

This famous jazz tune by Vince Guaraldi is heard in the 2015 film *The Peanuts Movie* and in many of the Peanuts animated specials on television, first appearing in 1964. Our abridged arrangement uses a simple pattern in the left hand, allowing you to concentrate on the melody in right hand. Choose a slow tempo to begin, increasing the tempo as you feel comfortable playing hands together. Observe the rests in measures 13–18. They give an energetic lift as well as contrast with the first theme.

Raiders March

Composed by John Williams for the 1981 film *Raiders of the Lost Ark*, "Raiders March" is sometimes called the "Indiana Jones" theme. This triumphant melody centers around the dotted quarter-eighth note, so give that eighth note a bit of a snap to move it along. Be on the lookout for accidentals, like the A♭ and D♭ in measures 11–12. John Williams adds quite a bit of color and excitement with unexpected harmonic shifts throughout this arrangement.

The Rainbow Connection

Kermit the Frog sings this delightful classic in the 1979 film *The Muppet Movie*, with music and lyrics by Paul Williams and Kenneth Ascher. You'll notice the tempo indication at the beginning of the song is "Flowing Waltz," and you'll want to keep that in mind as you play. Keep the melody gently moving with an ever so slight accent on beat one of each measure. The left-hand accompaniment starts out with broken chords in single notes, changing to a more typical waltz pattern in measure 39. In either case, play with a full, supportive tone but let the melody shine through.

Somewhere in My Memory

This gentle holiday song was composed by John Williams for the popular 1990 Christmas comedy, *Home Alone*. Really sing out with the right hand as you play this lyrical melody. Balance the left-hand accompaniment carefully. Be aware of the continuous two-note chords throughout; they should stay quietly supporting, with a full, round tone.

Somewhere Out There

This romantic ballad was written for the 1986 animated film *An American Tail*. During the film it was sung by brother and sister mice Fievel and Tanya Mousekewitz, and again over the end credits by Linda Ronstadt and James Ingram. That version was a hit on the Billboard Hot 100, reaching as high as the #2 spot. Feel free use a little rubato (push and pull) to convey the emotional quality of the lyrics; the eighth notes don't need to stay in a strict tempo. The slanted lines in measures 29–32 show the melody moving from treble to bass clef.

Speechless

Sung by the character Jasmine in the 2019 Disney live-action film *Aladdin*, "Speechless" is a powerful ballad. The song begins with a gently moving introduction, with both hands written in treble clef. As you play to the chorus in measure 21 the texture gets fuller, with two-note chords in the right hand, and, starting in measure 27, in the left hand. You may find it helpful to practice each hand separately at first. If you're unfamiliar with this song, listen to a recording from the movie soundtrack.

Star Wars (Main Theme)

This immediately recognizable theme by John Williams is heard at the beginning of every *Star Wars* film, starting with the first film (later subtitled *A New Hope*) in 1977. Triplets (three eighth notes played in the time of one quarter note) are a big part of this noble melody, so set your quarter note pulse carefully. This arrangement follows a simple A-B-A form, so once you reach measure 17 you return to material you've already learned.

Test Drive

From the 2010 animated motion picture *How to Train Your Dragon*, this dramatic selection from the film score is sometimes called the "flying" theme. You'll want the right hand to soar through the eighth notes, bringing this dramatic melody to life. Measures 7–10 are the same as measures 3–6, just an octave higher. Keep the eighth notes steady as you move up the keyboard. Accidentals (sharps and flats not in the key signature) and a key change (measure 48) add to the thrill and excitement, so enjoy taking this one out for a spin!

True Love's Kiss

This charming tune is from the 2007 Disney film *Enchanted*. The opening eight measures are played freely, almost as if speaking. After the fermatas in measure 8, settle right into a moderate tempo, but let the lyrics push and pull you along. There's a lot of movement in the left-hand accompaniment, so practice measures 8–15 with left hand alone. If you struggle to identify the notes, think about the intervals (distance between the notes) as you play from measure to measure. Once you're confident with the left hand, adding the right hand will be easier.

Try Everything

Sung by Shakira (as the character Gazelle) in the 2016 Walt Disney Animation Studios film *Zootopia*, this upbeat dance tune will have you singing along. Left hand provides a steady pulse to keep you on the beat while right-hand syncopation brings this song to life. Tap and count as you learn the melody and sing along. Don't be shy—try everything!

When She Loved Me

This sweet but melancholy tune was written by Randy Newman for the 1999 Pixar animated film *Toy Story 2* and was recorded by Sarah McLachlan. The melody should be played freely, with a singing right-hand tone and supportive left hand. Be aware of meter changes and fermatas but keep the quarter note pulse generally steady. Accidentals add poignant color to the harmony, so linger in those places that create tension and release.

Beyond the Sea

from FINDING NEMO

Lyrics by JACK LAWRENCE
Music by CHARLES TRENET and ALBERT LASRY
Original French Lyric to "La Mer" by CHARLES TRENET

be - yond a star; it's near be - yond the

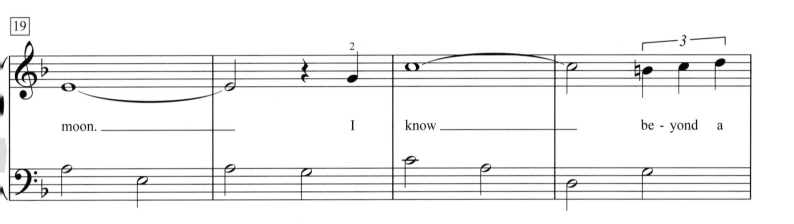

moon. _____ I know _____ be - yond a

D.S. al Coda

doubt, my heart will lead me there soon. _____ We'll

CODA

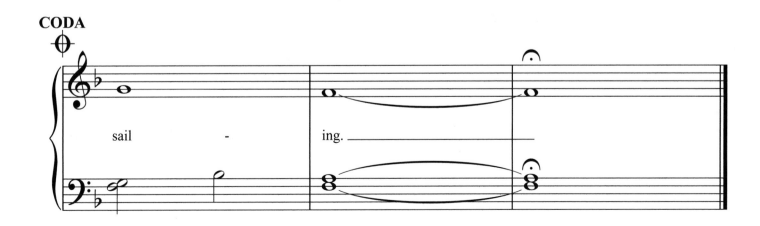

sail - ing. _____

Can't Stop the Feeling

from TROLLS

Words and Music by JUSTIN TIMBERLAKE,
MAX MARTIN and SHELLBACK

Moderate Funk groove

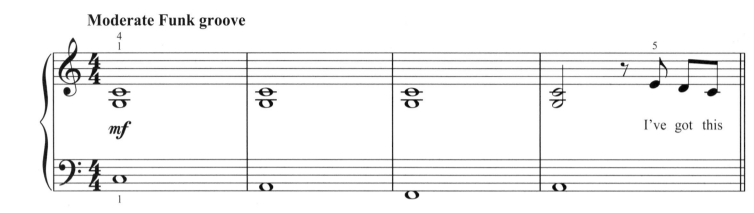

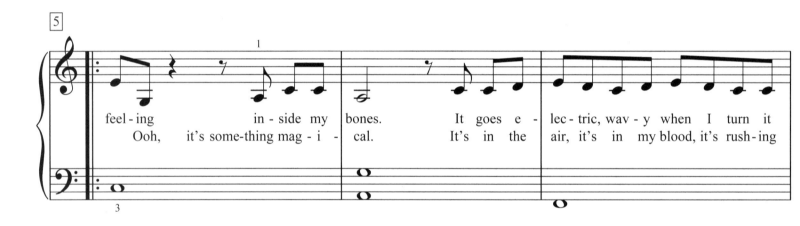

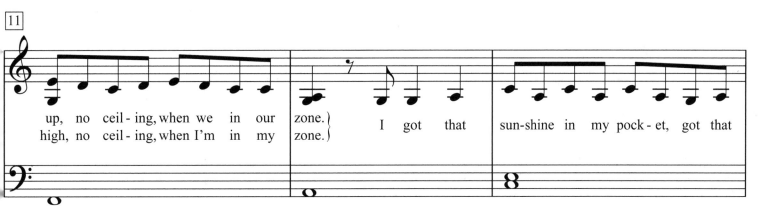

up, no ceil-ing, when we in our zone. high, no ceil-ing, when I'm in my zone. I got that sun-shine in my pock-et, got that

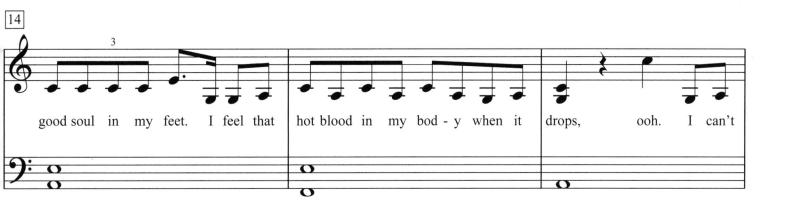

good soul in my feet. I feel that hot blood in my bod-y when it drops, ooh. I can't

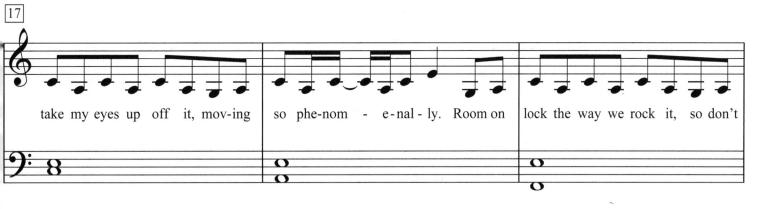

take my eyes up off it, mov-ing so phe-nom - e-nal-ly. Room on lock the way we rock it, so don't

stop. Un-der the lights when ev-'ry-thing goes, _____ no-where to

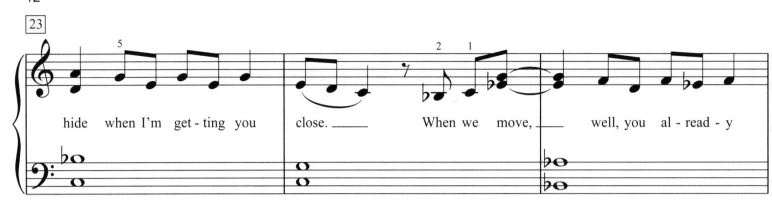

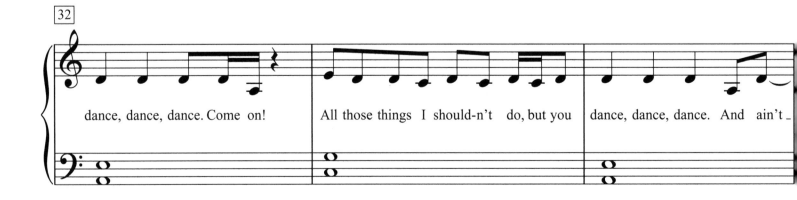

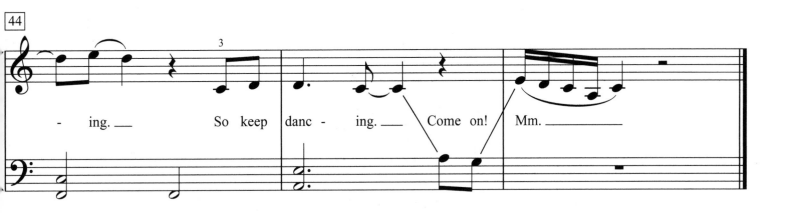

Theme from E.T.
(The Extra-Terrestrial)

from the Universal Picture E.T. (THE EXTRA TERRESTRIAL)

Music by JOHN WILLIAMS

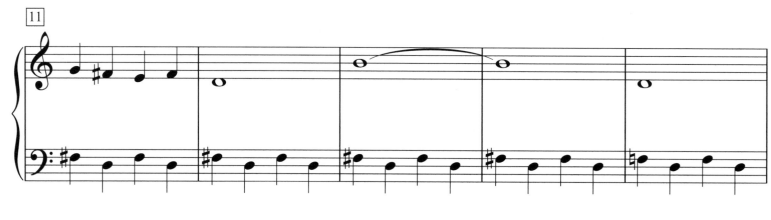

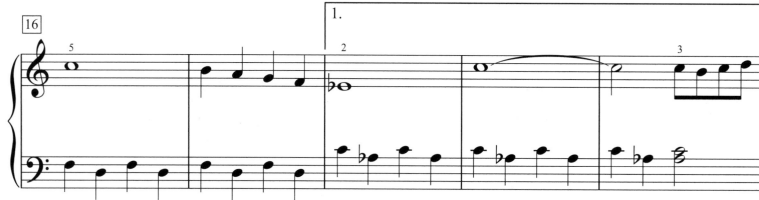

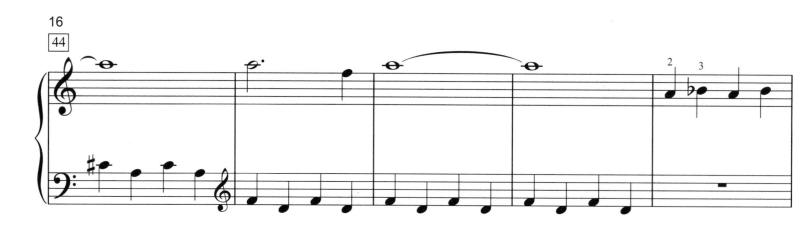

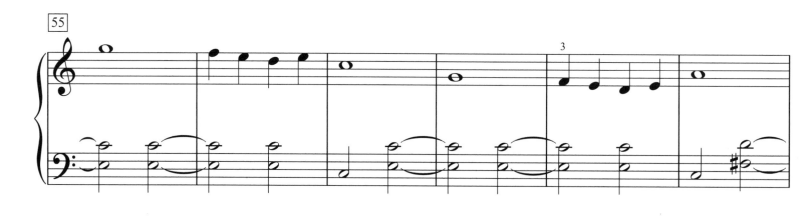

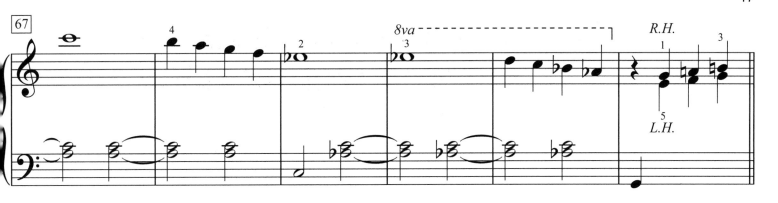

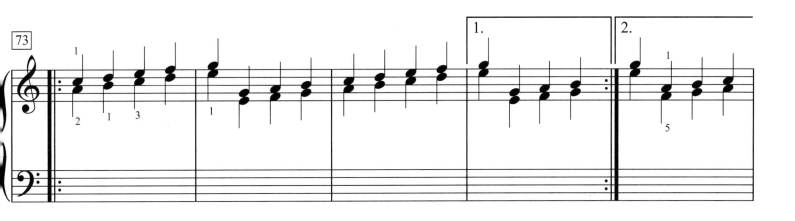

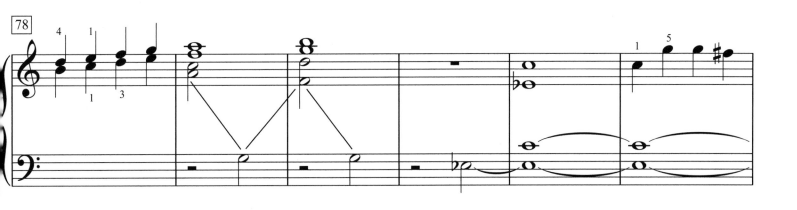

Everything Is Awesome
(Awesome Remixx!!!)

from THE LEGO MOVIE

Words by SHAWN PATTERSON
Music by ANDREW SAMBERG,
JORMA TACCONE, AKIVA SCHAFFER,
JOSHUA BARTHOLOMEW, LISA HARRITON
and SHAWN PATTERSON

Moderately fast

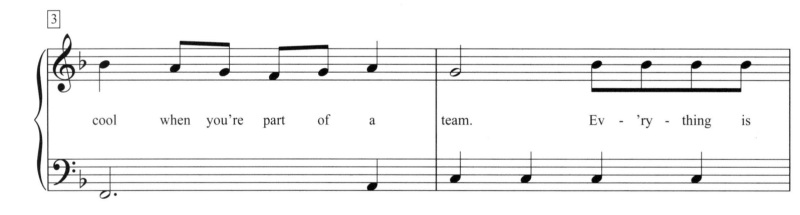

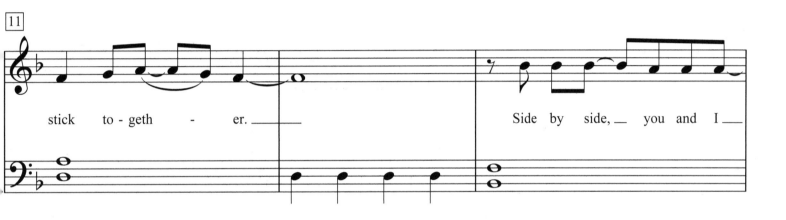

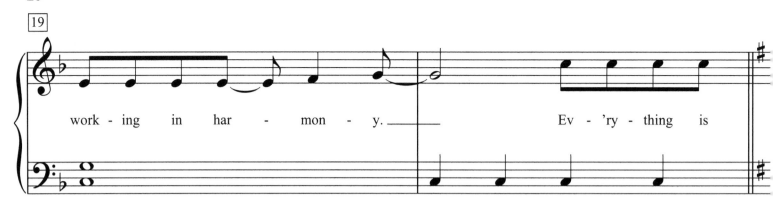

work - ing   in   har - mon - y._____   Ev - 'ry - thing is

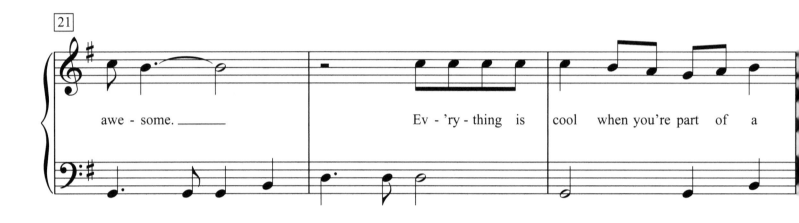

awe - some._____   Ev - 'ry - thing is cool when you're part of a

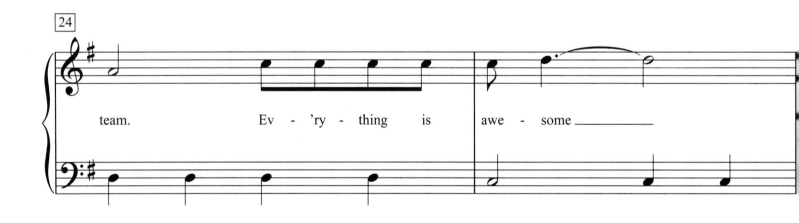

team.   Ev - 'ry - thing is   awe - some _____

when we're liv - ing the ____ dream.

How Far I'll Go

from MOANA

Music and Lyrics by
LIN-MANUEL MIRANDA

I've been __ star - ing at the edge of the wa-ter __ long __ as I can re-

mem - ber, __ nev - er real-ly know-ing why. I wish __ I could be the per-fect

daugh-ter, __ but I come back to the wa-ter __ no mat-ter how hard I try. Ev-'ry

go, there's just no tell-ing how far I'll go. I ___ know ___ ev-'ry-bod-y on this

is - land ___ seems ___ so hap-py on this is - land. ___ Ev -'ry-thing is by de - sign. ___

___ I know ___ ev -'ry-bod-y on this is - land ___ has ___ a role on this

is - land, ___ so may-be I can roll with mine. ___ I can lead with pride, I can make us strong. I'll be

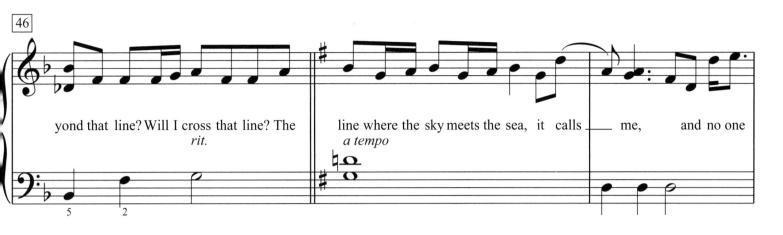

yond that line? Will I cross that line? The *rit.* line where the sky meets the sea, it calls ___ me, and no one

knows ___ how far it goes. ___ If the wind in my sail on the sea stays be - hind ___

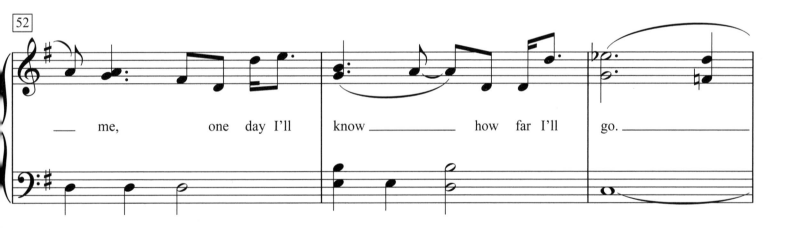

___ me, one day I'll know ___ how far I'll go. ___

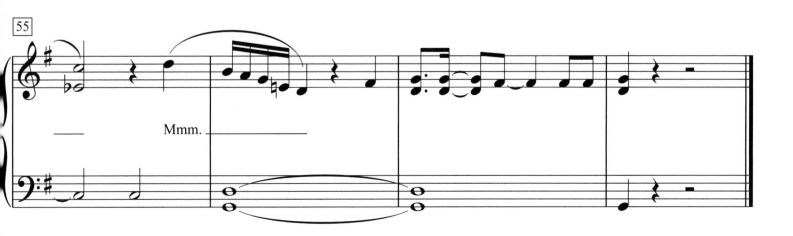

Mmm. ___

Happy

from DESPICABLE ME 2

Words and Music by
PHARRELL WILLIAMS

It   might   seem
Here   come   bad

cra - zy   what   I'm   'bout   to   say.
news, _   talk - in'   this   and   that.

Sun - shine, _   she's   here;   you   can   take   a   break.
Gim - me   all   you   got,   no ____   hold - ing   back.

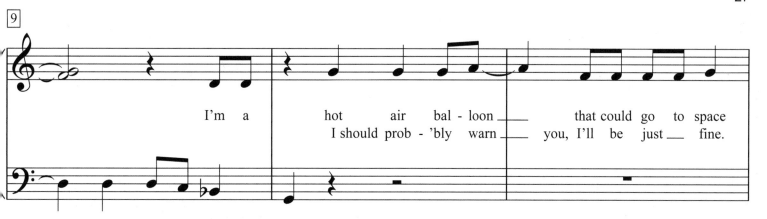

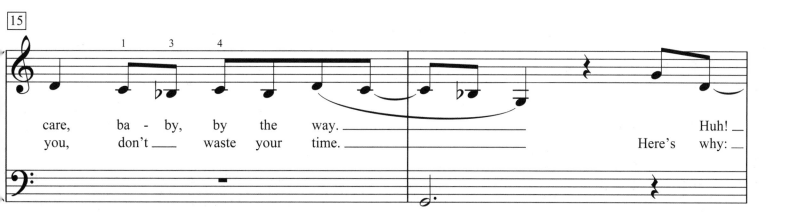

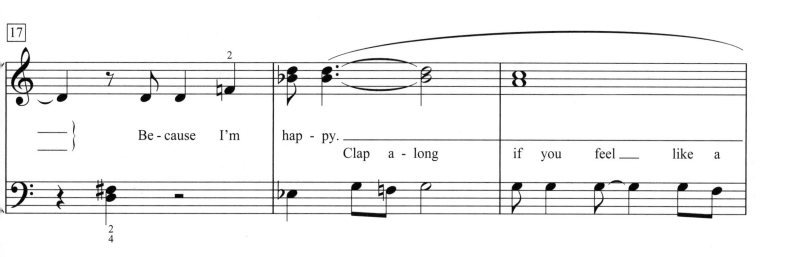

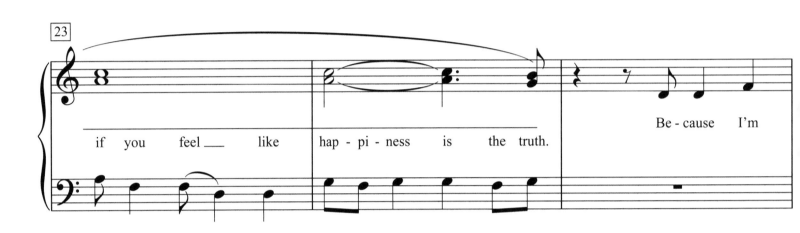

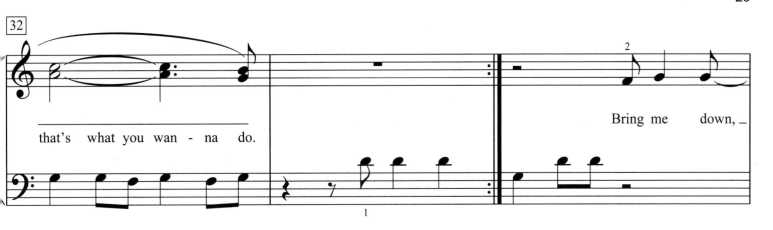

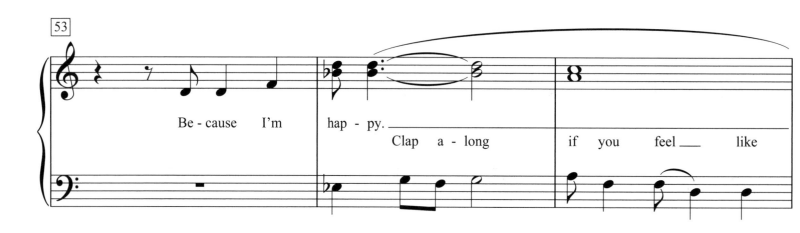

hap - pi - ness is the truth. Be - cause I'm hap - py. _____ Clap a - long _____

if you know ___ what hap - pi - ness is to you. Be - cause I'm

hap - py. _____ Clap a - long if you feel ___ like that's what you wan - na do.

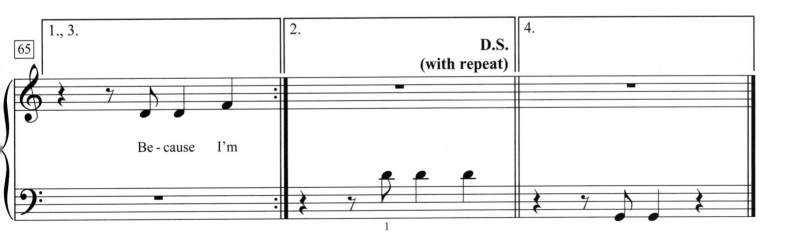

1., 3. Be - cause I'm

2. D.S. (with repeat)

4.

I See the Light

from TANGLED

Music by ALAN MENKEN
Lyrics by GLENN SLATER

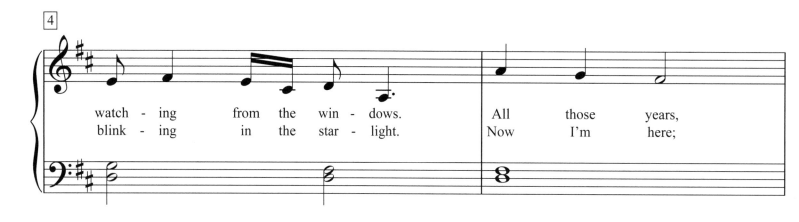

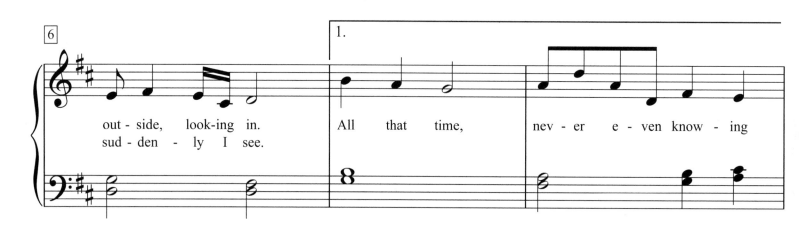

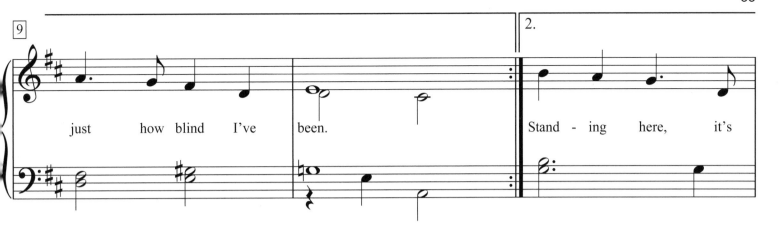

just how blind I've been. Stand - ing here, it's

oh, so clear I'm where I'm meant to be. And at

last I see the light, and it's like the fog has

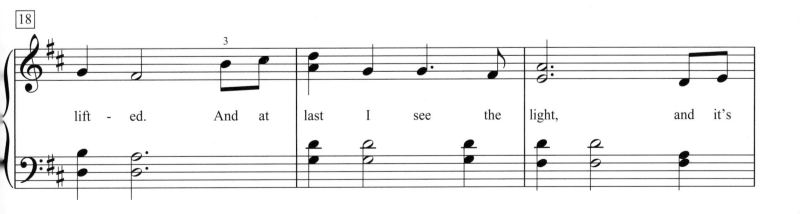

lift - ed. And at last I see the light, and it's

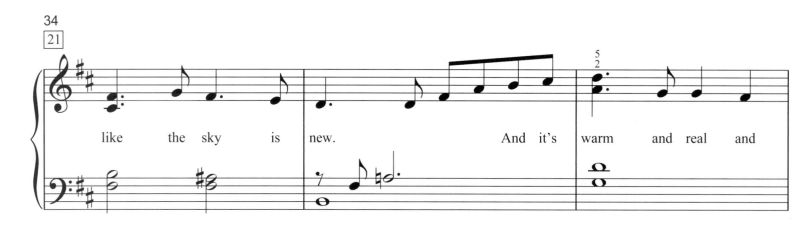

like the sky is new. And it's warm and real and

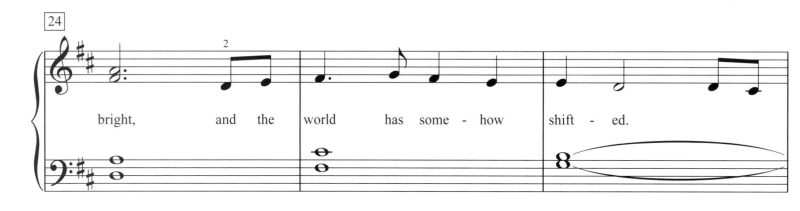

bright, and the world has some - how shift - ed.

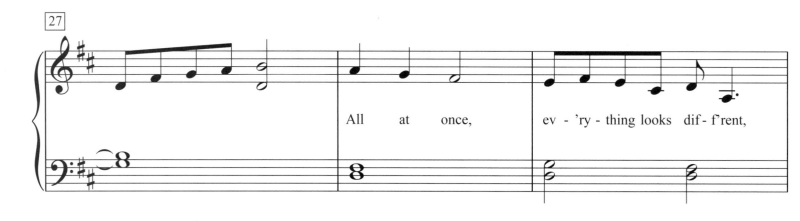

All at once, ev - 'ry - thing looks dif - f'rent,

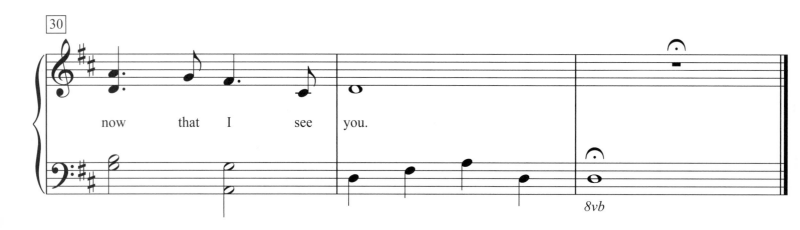

now that I see you.

8vb

Raiders March

from RAIDERS OF THE LOST ARK

Music by JOHN WILLIAMS

March tempo

36

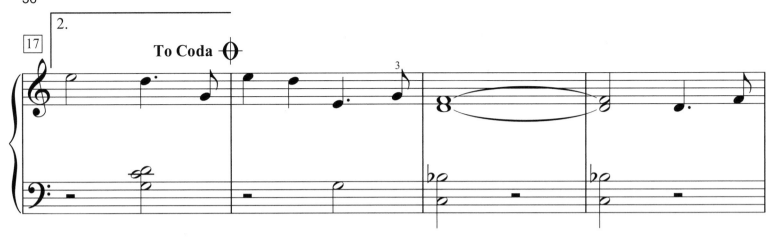

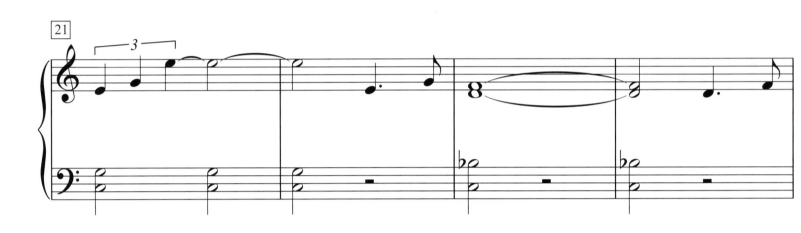

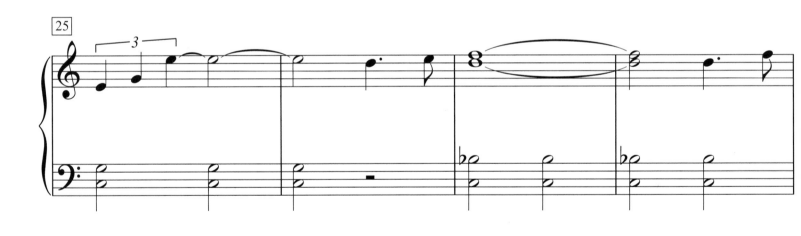

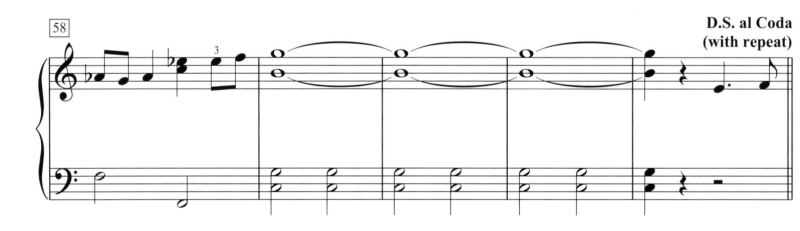

D.S. al Coda
(with repeat)

Immortals

from BIG HERO 6

Words and Music by ANDREW HURLEY,
JOE TROHMAN, PATRICK STUMP
and PETE WENTZ

sand in the bot-tom half of the hour - glass, glass, glass. Oh, _____

_____ I'll try to pic-ture me with-out you but I can't. 'Cause we could be im-

or - tals, i - i - i - i - im - mor - tals. Just not for long, __ for

long. And live with me for - ev - er now, you pull the black-out cur - tains down. __ Just

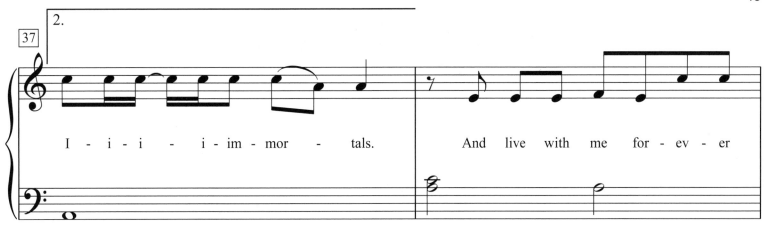

I - i - i - i - i - im - mor - tals. And live with me for - ev - er

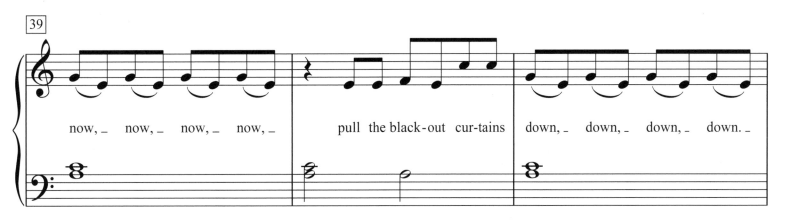

now, _ now, _ now, _ now, _ pull the black-out cur-tains down, _ down, _ down, _ down. _

We could be im - mor - tals, i - i - i - i - im -

D.S. al Coda

CODA

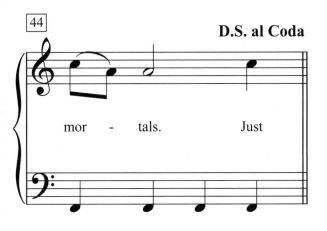

mor - tals. Just

i - i - i - i - i - im - mor - tals.

rit.

Into the Unknown

from FROZEN 2

Music and Lyrics by KRISTEN ANDERSON-LOPEZ
and ROBERT LOPEZ

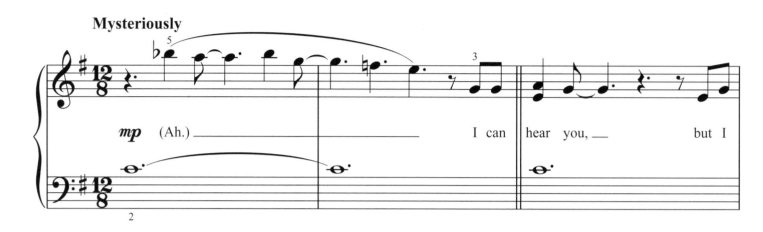

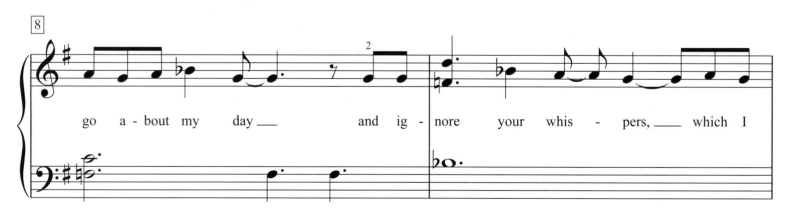

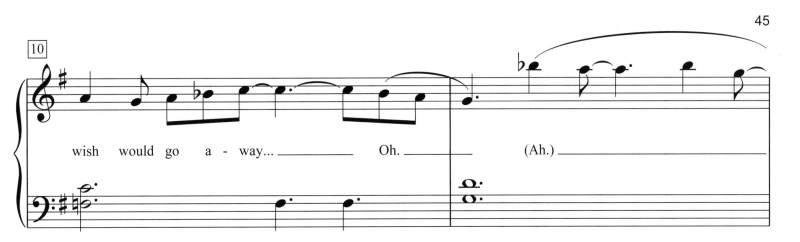

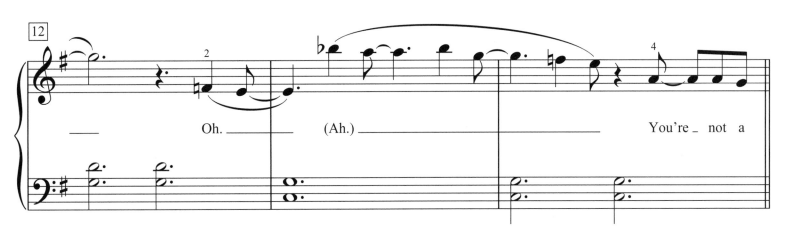

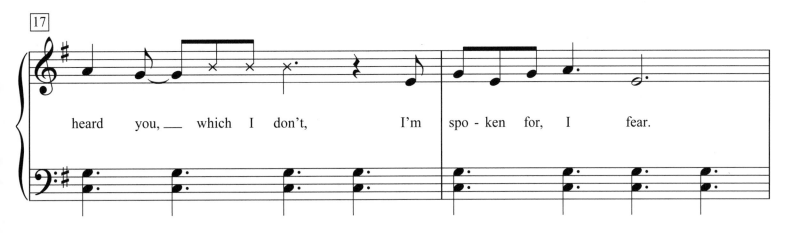

Ev - 'ry-one I've ev - er loved is here with-in these walls. _ I'm

sor - ry, se - cret si - ren, but I'm block-ing out your calls. _ I've

had my ad - ven - ture. _ I don't need some-thing new! _ I'm a-

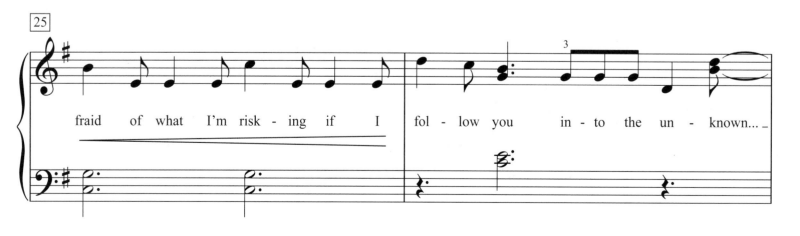

fraid of what I'm risk-ing if I fol - low you in - to the un - known... _

in - to the un - known,

in - to the un - known!

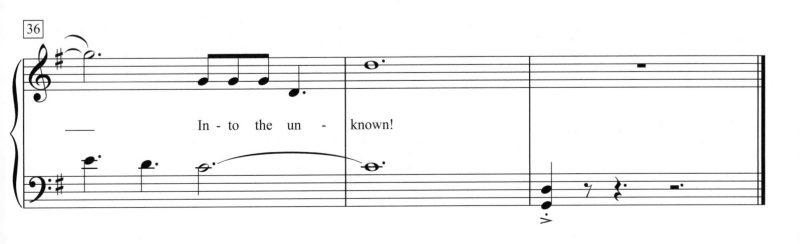

(Ah, _____ ah.) _____

In - to the un - known!

Linus and Lucy

from THE PEANUTS MOVIE

By VINCE GUARALDI

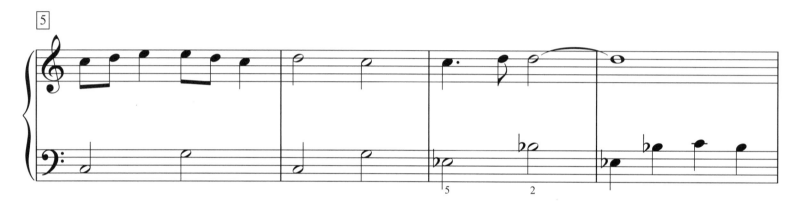

The Rainbow Connection

from THE MUPPET MOVIE

Words and Music by PAUL WILLIAMS
and KENNETH L. ASCHER

Flowing Waltz

Why are there so man - y songs a - bout
Who said that ev - 'ry wish would be heard and
Have you been half a - sleep and have you heard

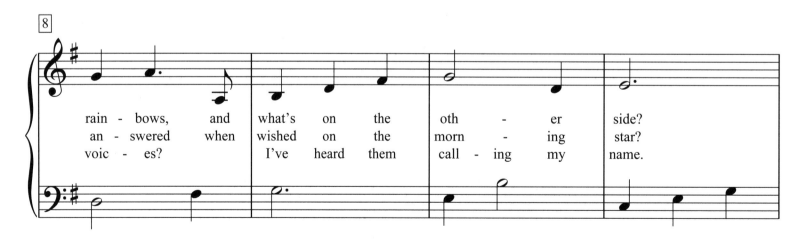

rain - bows, and what's on the oth - er side?
an - swered and when wished on the morn - ing star?
voic - es? I've heard them call - ing my name.

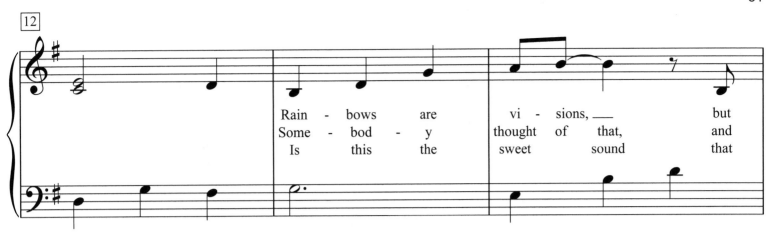

Rain - bows are vi - sions, _____ but
Some - bod - y thought of that, and
Is this the sweet sound and that

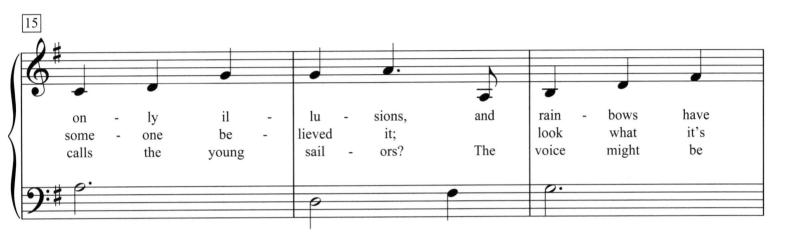

on - ly il - lu - sions, and rain - bows have
some - one be - lieved it; look what it's
calls the young sail - ors? The voice might be

noth - ing to hide. So we've been
done _____ so so far. What's so a -
one and the same. I've heard it

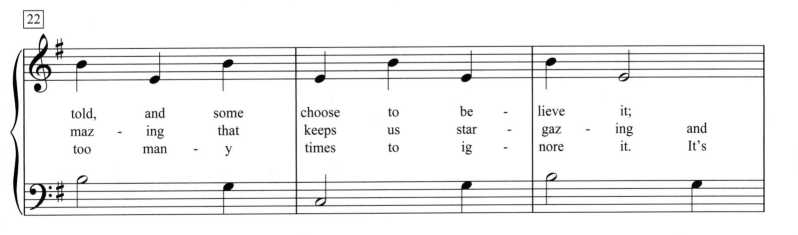

told, and some choose to be - lieve it;
maz - ing that keeps us star - gaz - ing and
too man - y times to ig - nore it. It's

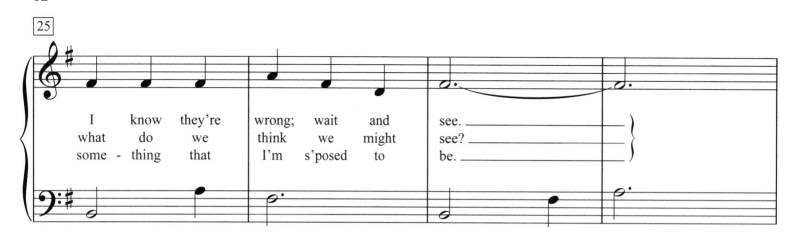

I know they're wrong; wait and see. _____
what do we think we might see? _____
some-thing that I'm s'posed to be. _____

Some-day we'll find it, the Rain-bow Con - nec - tion; the

To Coda ⊕

1.

lov-ers, the dream-ers ___ and me.

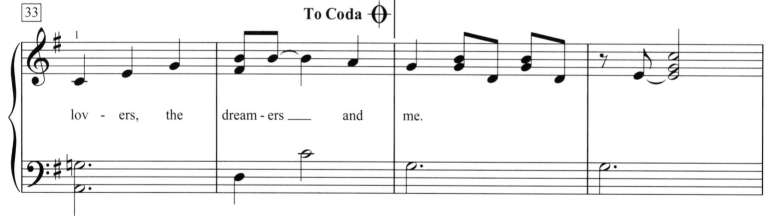

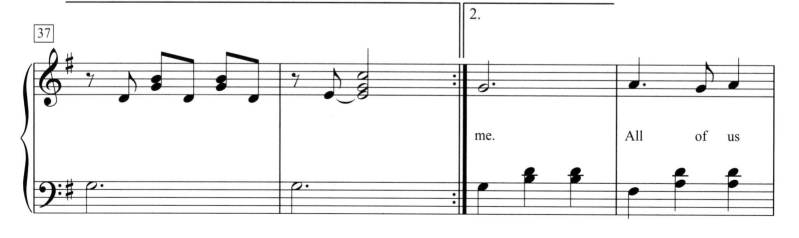

2.

me. All of us

41

un - der its spell; we know that it's prob - a - bly

45

D.S. al Coda

CODA

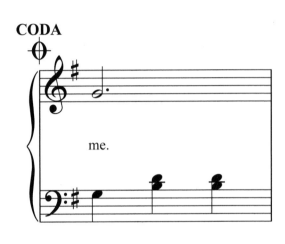

mag - ic.

me.

48

La da da de da da do la

51

la da da da de da do._____

Somewhere in My Memory

from the Twentieth Century Fox Motion Picture HOME ALONE

Words by LESLIE BRICUSSE
Music by JOHN WILLIAMS

Gently

Can - dles in the

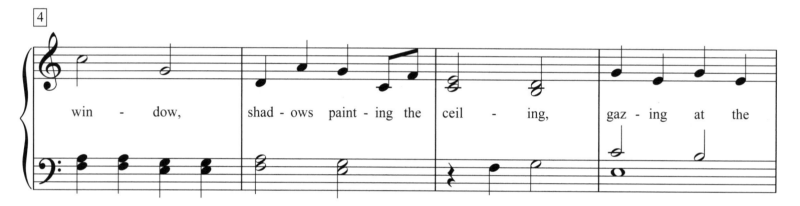

win - dow,　shad - ows paint - ing the　ceil - ing,　gaz - ing at the

fire　glow,　feel - ing that "gin - ger - bread"　feel - ing.

Pre - cious mo - ments,　spe - cial peo - ple,　hap - py fac - es

Somewhere Out There

from AN AMERICAN TAIL

Music by BARRY MANN
and JAMES HORNER
Lyric by CYNTHIA WEIL

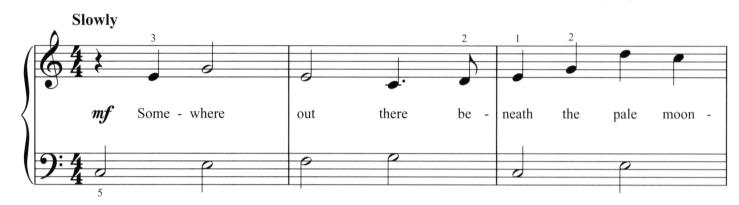

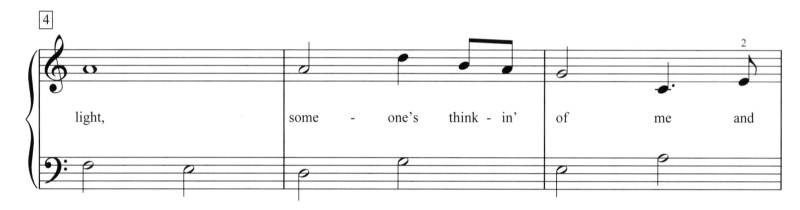

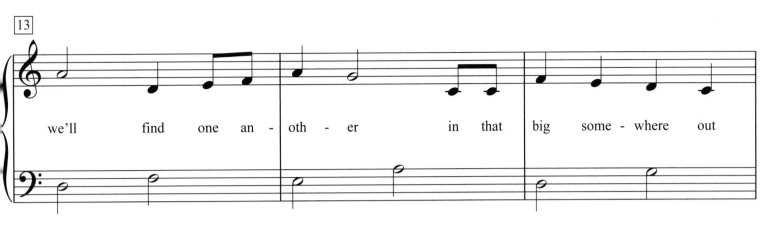

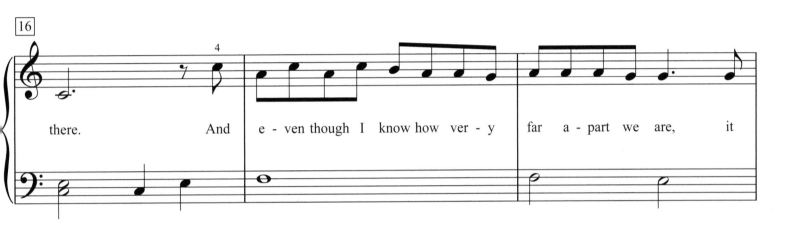

neath the same big sky.

rit.

Some - where out there, if

a tempo

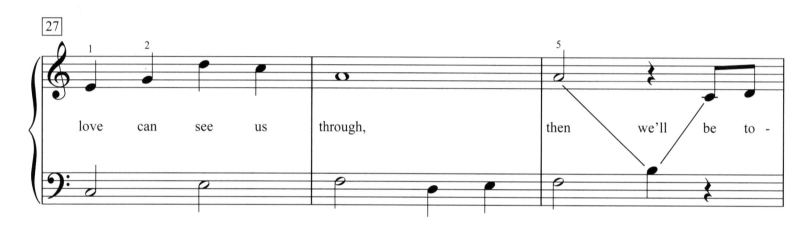

love can see us through, then we'll be to -

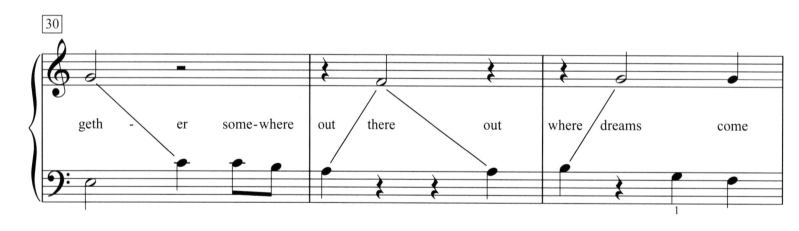

geth - er some-where out there out where dreams come

true. _____

rit.

Speechless

from ALADDIN 2019

Music by ALAN MENKEN
Lyrics by BENJ PASEK
and JUSTIN PAUL

Half-time feel

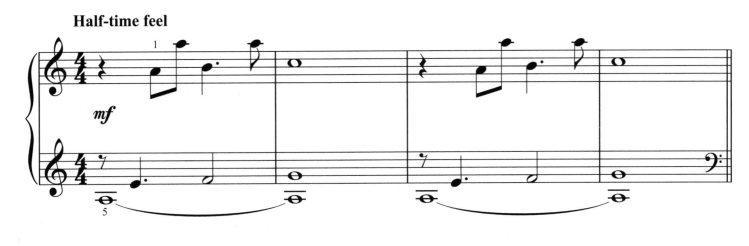

Here comes a wave meant to wash me a-way, a tide that is tak-ing me un-

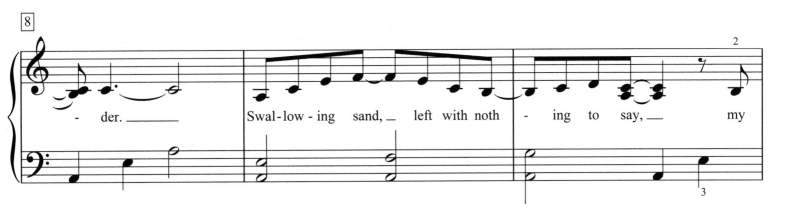

-der. Swal-low-ing sand, left with noth - ing to say, my

voice drowned out in the thun - der. But I won't cry, and

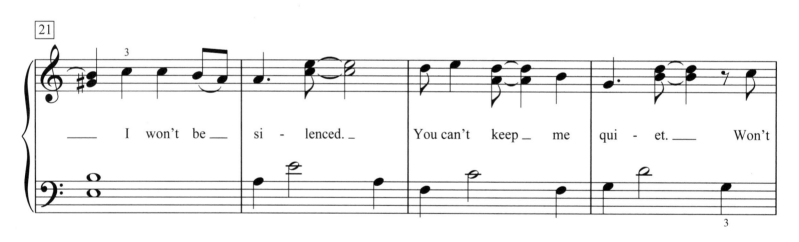

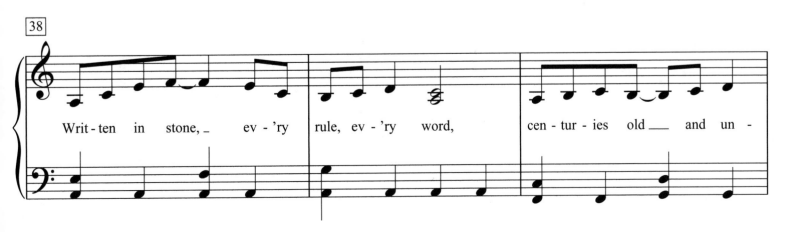

You can't keep me qui - et. Won't trem - ble when you try it. All I know

is I won't go speech - less. All I know is I won't go speech -

- less. Speech - less! _

Star Wars (Main Theme)

from STAR WARS: A NEW HOPE

Music by JOHN WILLIAMS

Majestically

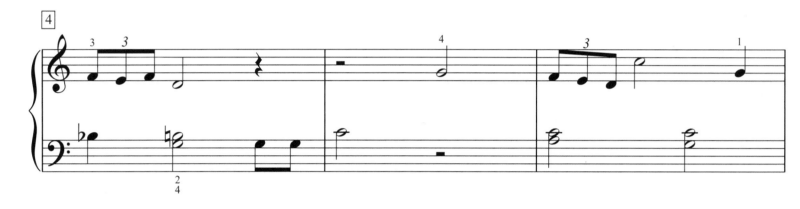

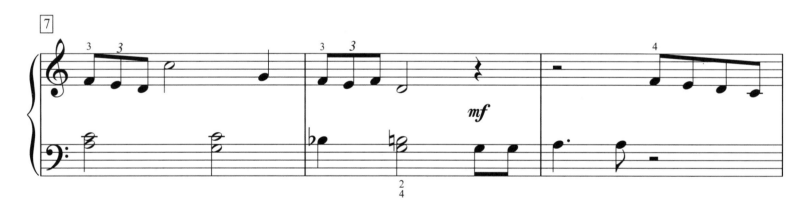

Test Drive

from the Motion Picture HOW TO TRAIN YOUR DRAGON

By JOHN POWELL

Moderately fast

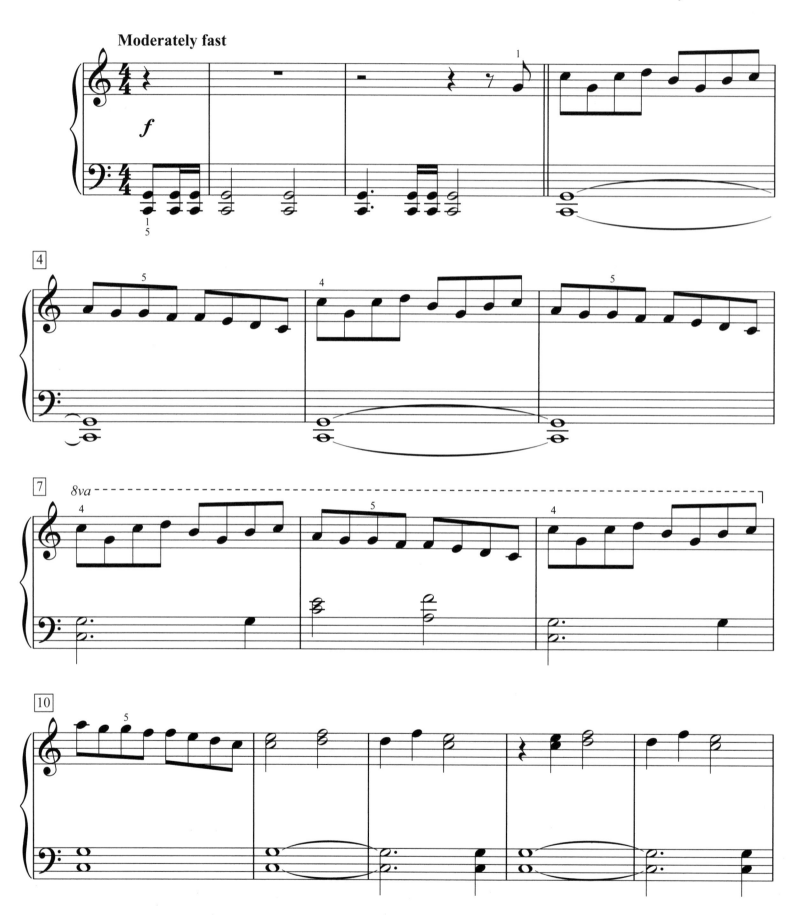

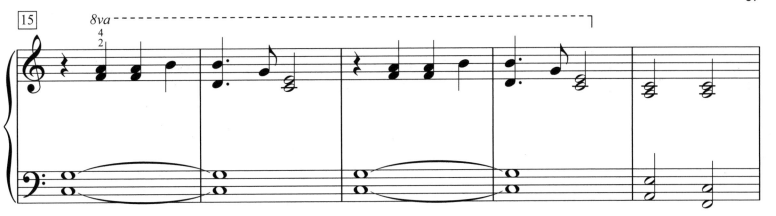

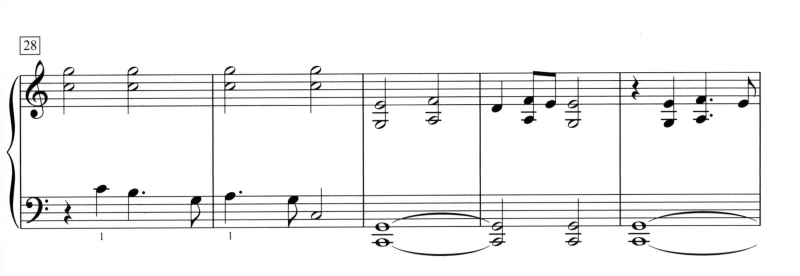

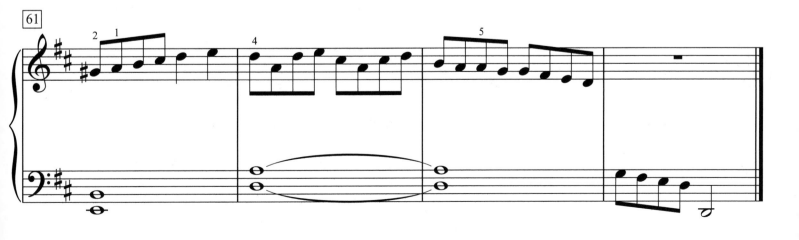

True Love's Kiss

from ENCHANTED

Music by ALAN MENKEN
Lyrics by STEPHEN SCHWARTZ

Easily, with freedom

When you meet the some - one who was meant for you, be - fore two can be - come one, there's

some-thing you must do.

More flowing, still freely

There is some-thing sweet - er ev - 'ry-bod - y needs. I've been dream-ing of a

true love's kiss; and a prince I'm hop - ing comes with this.

That's what brings ev - er - af - ter - ings so hap - py. And

that's the rea - son we need lips so much, for lips are the on - ly

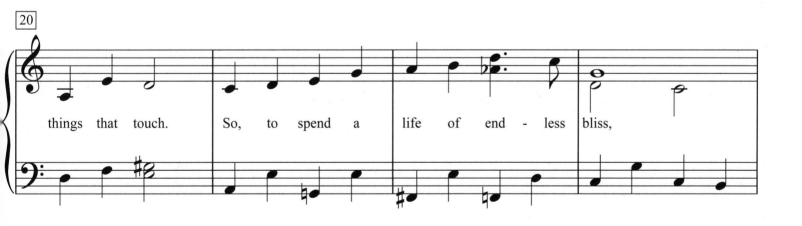

things that touch. So, to spend a life of end - less bliss,

just find who you love through true love's kiss.

Try Everything

from ZOOTOPIA

Words and Music by SIA FURLER,
TOR ERIK HERMANSEN and MIKKEL ERIKSEN

Moderate Dance beat

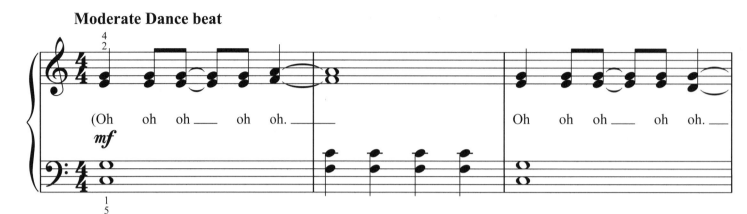

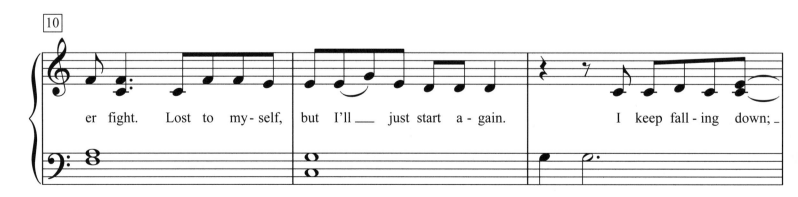

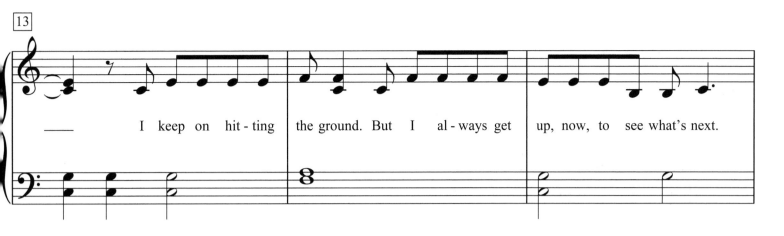

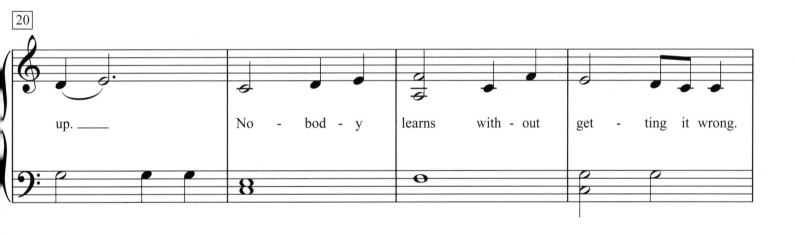

ven though I could fail.

Oh oh oh ___ oh oh. ___

___ Try ev-'ry-thing. ___

Oh oh oh ___ oh oh. ___

Try ev-'ry-thing. ___

Oh oh oh ___ oh oh. ___

Try ev-'ry-thing. ___

Oh oh oh ___ oh oh. ___

___

Try ev-'ry-thing. ___

When She Loved Me

from TOY STORY 2

Music and Lyrics by
RANDY NEWMAN

Tenderly, freely

When some - bod - y loved me, ev - 'ry - thing was beau - ti - ful.

mf

Ev - 'ry hour we spent to - geth - er lives with - in my heart. And when she was sad,

I was there to dry her tears; and when she was hap - py, so was I, when

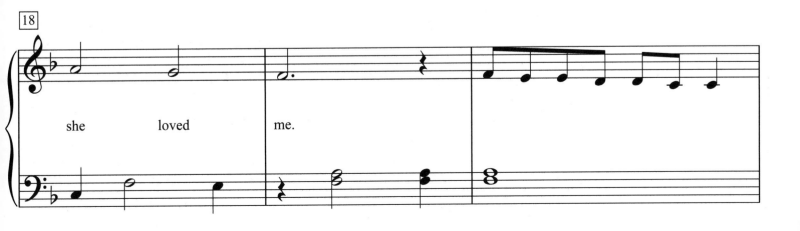

So the years went by; I stayed the same. But

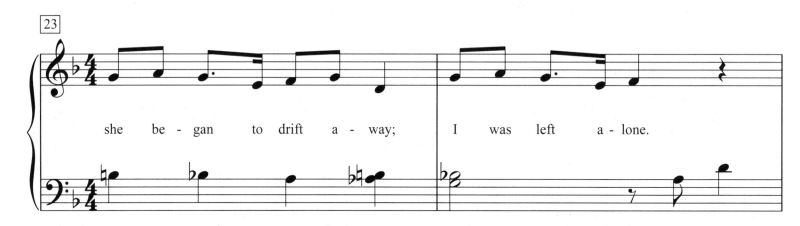

she be - gan to drift a - way; I was left a - lone.

Still I wait - ed for the day when she'd say, "I will al - ways

love you." Lone - ly and for - got - ten, nev - er thought she'd look my way, and she

smiled at me and held me just like she used to do, like she

loved me when she loved me. When some-bod-y loved me,

ev-'ry-thing was beau-ti-ful. Ev-'ry hour we spent to-geth-er lives with-in my heart, when

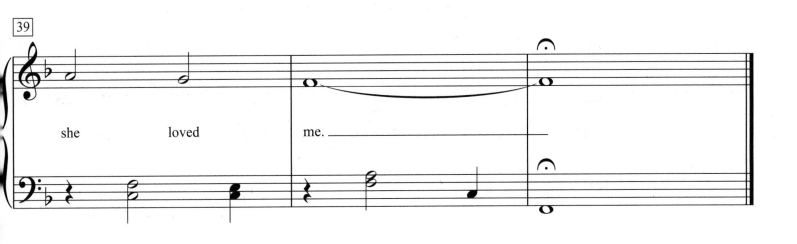

she loved me.

It's Easy to Play Your Favorite Songs with Hal Leonard Easy Piano Books

The Best Praise & Worship Songs Ever

The name says it all: over 70 of the best P&W songs today. Titles include: Awesome God • Blessed Be Your Name • Come, Now Is the Time to Worship • Days of Elijah • Here I Am to Worship • Open the Eyes of My Heart • Shout to the Lord • We Fall Down • and more.
00311312 .... $19.99

First 50 Popular Songs You Should Play on the Piano

50 great pop classics for beginning pianists to learn, including: Candle in the Wind • Chopsticks • Don't Know Why • Hallelujah • Happy Birthday to You • Heart and Soul • I Walk the Line • Just the Way You Are • Let It Be • Let It Go • Over the Rainbow • Piano Man • and many more.
00131140 .... $16.99

The Greatest Video Game Music

28 easy piano selections for the music that envelops you as you lose yourself in the world of video games, including: Angry Birds Theme • Assassin's Creed Revelations • Dragonborn (Skyrim Theme) • Elder Scrolls: Oblivion • Minecraft: Sweden • Rage of Sparta from God of War III • and more.
00202545 .... $17.99

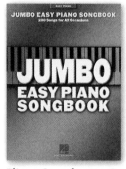

Jumbo Easy Piano Songbook

200 classical favorites, folk songs and jazz standards. Includes: Amazing Grace • Beale Street Blues • Bridal Chorus • Buffalo Gals • Canon in D • Cielito Lindo • Danny Boy • The Entertainer • Für Elise • Greensleeves • Jamaica Farewell • Marianne • Molly Malone • Ode to Joy • Peg O' My Heart • Rockin' Robin • Yankee Doodle • dozens more!
00311014 .... $19.99

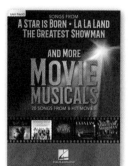

Songs from A Star Is Born, The Greatest Showman, La La Land, and More Movie Musicals

Movie musical lovers will delight in this songbook chock full of top-notch songs arranged for easy piano with lyrics from blockbuster movies. Includes: City of Stars from *La La Land* • Suddenly from *Les Misérables* • This Is Me from *The Greatest Showman* • Shallow from *A Star Is Born* • and more.
00287577 .... $17.99

50 Easy Classical Themes

Easy arrangements of 50 classical tunes representing more than 30 composers, including: Bach, Beethoven, Chopin, Debussy, Dvorak, Handel, Haydn, Liszt, Mozart, Mussorgsky, Puccini, Rossini, Schubert, Strauss, Tchaikovsky, Vivaldi, and more.
00311215 .... $14.99

Pop Songs for Kids

Kids from all corners of the world love and sing along to the songs of Taylor Swift, One Direction, Katy Perry, and other pop stars. This collection features 25 songs from these and many more artists in easy piano format. Includes: Brave • Can't Stop the Feeling • Firework • Home • Let It Go • Shake It Off • What Makes You Beautiful • and more.
00221920 .... $14.99

Simple Songs – The Easiest Easy Piano Songs

Play 50 of your favorite songs in the easiest of arrangements! Songs include: Castle on a Cloud • Do-Re-Mi • Happy Birthday to You • Hey Jude • Let It Go • Linus and Lucy • Over the Rainbow • Smile • Star Wars (Main Theme) • Tomorrow • and more.
00142041 .... $14.99

VH1's 100 Greatest Songs of Rock and Roll

The results from the VH1 show that featured the 100 greatest rock and roll songs of all time are here in this awesome collection! Songs include: Born to Run • Good Vibrations • Hey Jude • Hotel California • Imagine • Light My Fire • Like a Rolling Stone • Respect • and more.
00311110 .... $29.99

River Flows in You and Other Eloquent Songs for Easy Piano Solo

24 piano favorites arranged so that even beginning players can sound great. Includes: All of Me • Bella's Lullaby • Cristofori's Dream • Il Postino (The Postman) • Jessica's Theme (Breaking in the Colt) • The John Dunbar Theme • and more.
00137581 .... $14.99

Disney's My First Song Book

16 favorite songs to sing and play. Every page is beautifully illustrated with full-color art from Disney features. Songs include: Beauty and the Beast • Bibbidi-Bobbidi-Boo • Circle of Life • Cruella De Vil • A Dream Is a Wish Your Heart Makes • Hakuna Matata • Under the Sea • Winnie the Pooh • You've Got a Friend in Me • and more.
00310322 .... $17.99

Top Hits of 2019

20 of the year's best are included in this collection arranged for easy piano with lyrics. Includes: Bad Guy (Billie Eilish) • I Don't Care (Ed Sheeran & Justin Bieber) • ME! (Taylor Swift feat. Brendon Urie) • Old Town Road (Remix) (Lil Nas X feat. Billy Ray Cyrus) • Senorita (Shawn Mendes & Camila Cabello) • Someone You Loved (Lewis Capaldi) • and more.
00302273 .... $16.99

Get complete song lists and more at
www.halleonard.com

Prices, contents, and availability subject to change without notice
Disney characters and artwork © Disney Enterprises, Inc.

HAL•LEONARD®

0320
239